It's show time, SNOOPY

Selected Cartoons from
SPEAK SOFTLY, AND CARRY A BEAGLE, Vol. II

by CHARLES M. SCHULZ

FAWCETT CREST • NEW YORK

IT'S SHOW TIME, SNOOPY

This book, prepared especially for Fawcett Crest Books, a unit of CBS Publications, the Consumer Publishing Division of CBS Inc. comprises a portion of *SPEAK SOFTLY, AND CARRY A BEAGLE* and is reprinted by arrangement with Holt, Rinehart and Winston.

Contents of Book

ISBN: 0-449-23602-1

Printed in the United States of America

20 19 18 17 16 15 14 13 12 11

It's
show time,
SNOOPY

MORE PEANUTS®

(in editions with brightly colored pages)

☐ A BOY NAMED CHARLIE BROWN   23217 $2.25

☐ SNOOPY AND HIS SOPWITH CAMEL   23799 $1.75

☐ SNOOPY AND THE RED BARON   23719 $1.75

☐ THE "SNOOPY, COME HOME"
    MOVIE BOOK   23726 $1.95